The Power of Hallucinogens

The Power of Hallucinogens

A Guide to the History and Use of Psychedelics, Including LSD, Psilocybin (Magic Mushrooms), Mescaline (Peyote), DMT, and Ayahuasca

Journey into the Psychedelic Mind
Book 1

Terence Wright

Book
Bound Studios

Copyright © 2022 by Terence Wright

All rights reserved. No part of this book may be reproduced, stored in a retrieval system, or transmitted in any form or by any means, electronic, mechanical, photocopying, recording, or otherwise, without the prior written permission of the publisher, Book Bound Studios.

The information contained in this book is based on the author's personal experiences and research. While every effort has been made to ensure the accuracy of the information presented, the author and publisher cannot be held responsible for any errors or omissions. The information in this book is not intended as medical or legal advice, and should not be used as such.

This book is intended for general informational purposes only and is not a substitute for professional medical or legal advice. If you have specific questions about any medical or legal matters, you should consult with a qualified healthcare professional or attorney.

Book Bound Studios is not affiliated with any product or vendor mentioned in this book. The views expressed in this book are those of the author and do not necessarily reflect the views of Book Bound Studios.

To my family and friends, who have always supported me in my endeavors.

To the indigenous cultures that have long recognized the power of these substances and to the early researchers who dared to study them.

And to the countless individuals who have had profound and transformative experiences through the use of these substances, this book is dedicated.

Terence Wright

"It is the chief characteristic of the religion of science that it works, and that it works no otherwise than as a machine works."

— Thomas Henry Huxley

Contents

Foreword	xi
Introduction	xiii

1. LYSERGIC ACID DIETHYLAMIDE (LSD) — 1
- Chemical Structure and Effects on the Brain — 2
- History and Cultural Significance — 4
- Risks and Potential Therapeutic Uses — 6
- A Guide to Taking LSD — 7
- Chapter Summary — 9

2. PSILOCYBIN — 11
- Chemical Structure and Effects on the Brain — 12
- History and Cultural Significance — 14
- Risks and Potential Therapeutic Uses — 15
- A Guide to Taking Psilocybin — 16
- Chapter Summary — 19

3. MESCALINE (PEYOTE) — 21
- Chemical Structure and Effects on the Brain — 22
- History and Cultural Significance — 23
- Risks and Potential Therapeutic Uses — 25
- A Guide to Taking Mescaline — 26
- Chapter Summary — 28

4. N,N-DIMETHYLTRYPTAMINE (DMT) — 29
- Chemical Structure and Effects on the Brain — 30
- History and Cultural Significance — 32
- Risks and Potential Therapeutic Uses — 33
- A Guide to Taking DMT — 35
- Chapter Summary — 36

5. AYAHUASCA — 39
  Chemical Structure and Effects on the Brain — 40
  History and Cultural Significance — 42
  Risks and Potential Therapeutic Uses — 43
  A Guide to Taking Ayahuasca — 45
  Chapter Summary — 47

6. PERSONAL STORIES — 49
  Stories About LSD — 50
  Stories About Psilocybin — 53
  Stories About Peyote — 56
  Stories About DMT — 59
  Stories About Ayahuasca — 62

Afterword — 67
Acknowledgments — 73
About the Author — 75

Foreword

Terence Wright takes us on a journey into hallucinogens, exploring their rich history, cultural significance, potential therapeutic benefits and a guide to taking them safely in this groundbreaking book. With a deep understanding of the subject matter and a clear writing style, he guides us through the complex and often misunderstood world of psychedelics.

Wright's research is thorough, and his analysis is insightful. He presents a balanced and nuanced view of these substances, drawing on scientific research and personal accounts to provide a comprehensive understanding of their impact on the mind and society.

The book is a must-read for anyone interested in hallucinogens' history, science, and cultural significance. It is also an important resource for professionals in the field of mental health, providing a wealth of information on the potential therapeutic uses of these substances.

With this book, Wright has made an important contribution to the field of psychedelics research. His work will be of great value to researchers, clinicians, and anyone interested in understanding the power of these fascinating substances.

Introduction

Hallucinogens, also referred to as psychedelics, are a unique class of psychoactive substances utilized in various cultures throughout history for spiritual and medicinal purposes. These powerful compounds alter perceptions, thoughts, and emotions, often leading to profound and transformative experiences.

Introduction

In this book, we delve into the rich history, effects, and cultural significance of five specific hallucinogens: lysergic acid diethylamide (LSD), psilocybin, mescaline (peyote), N,N-dimethyltryptamine (DMT), and ayahuasca. Each of these substances has unique characteristics and has been used in different ways throughout history. We will explore the scientific and historical aspects of each of these substances, from their discovery and early research to their current uses and potential future applications. We will also look at these substances' cultural and spiritual significance, from their traditional use in indigenous societies to their current use in modern spiritual and therapeutic settings. Finally, we look at a simple guide to taking these psychedelics safely.

We will delve deeper into the effects of these substances on the brain and their potential therapeutic uses, such as for treating addiction, PTSD, and depression. We will also explore their use's risks and side effects and the current legal and policy implications. The book will also feature personal stories and accounts of individuals who have used these substances, providing a unique perspective on their effects and potential benefits.

The book aims to comprehensively understand hallucinogens, shedding light on their complex history, cultural significance, effects, and potential therapeutic uses. In addition, it aims to provide readers with an in-depth understanding of these fascinating substances and the potential they hold for the field of mental health and well-being.

Definition and Background of Hallucinogens

Hallucinogens are a diverse group of psychoactive compounds that can alter an individual's perceptions, thoughts, and emotions. They can be derived from various sources, including plants and animals, and even synthesized in a laboratory. Consequently, the

Introduction

effects of these substances can vary greatly depending on the substance consumed, the dosage, and the individual's state of mind.

Hallucinogens have been used for centuries in various cultures for spiritual and medicinal purposes. The earliest use of hallucinogens dates back to prehistory, with psychoactive substances in ritual and spiritual practices well-documented in many ancient cultures. Traditional medicine has also used these substances for their believed healing properties.

Hallucinogens can be divided into two main categories: classic psychedelics and dissociative psychedelics. Classic psychedelics include lysergic acid diethylamide (LSD), psilocybin, and mescaline (peyote), which enhance sensory experiences and increase emotions. In contrast, dissociative psychedelics such as ketamine disrupt the brain's normal functioning and alter the sense of reality.

The effects of hallucinogens on the brain and how they affect perception thought, and emotion still needs to be fully understood. However, recent research has begun to shed light on the mechanisms by which these substances affect the brain. For example, studies have shown that hallucinogens can increase activity in certain brain regions and disrupt the normal functioning of neural networks, leading to changes in perception, thought, and emotion.

Overall, the term "hallucinogen" encompasses various psychoactive compounds used for centuries in various cultures for spiritual and medicinal purposes. Their effects can vary depending on the substance, dosage, and the individual's state of mind. Despite their historical use, our understanding of these substances' effects and mechanisms of action still needs to be improved. More research is needed to understand their potential therapeutic benefits and risks fully.

Introduction

Overview of the Five Hallucinogens Discussed in this Book

Hallucinogens, also known as psychedelics, have been used for centuries for spiritual and medicinal purposes. These powerful compounds alter perceptions, thoughts, and emotions, often leading to profound and transformative experiences. In this book, we will explore the history, effects, and cultural significance of five specific hallucinogens: lysergic acid diethylamide (LSD), psilocybin, mescaline (peyote), N,N-dimethyltryptamine (DMT), and ayahuasca. Each of these substances has unique characteristics and has been used in different ways throughout history.

In this chapter, we will delve into the specific properties of these substances. We will begin by exploring LSD, a synthetic compound developed in 1938 and known for its powerful and long-lasting hallucinations. We will then move on to psilocybin, a naturally occurring psychedelic compound found in certain mushrooms, which has been used for centuries by indigenous cultures for spiritual and medicinal purposes and is being studied for its potential therapeutic uses in treating conditions such as depression, anxiety, and PTSD.

We will also examine mescaline, a psychoactive alkaloid found in the peyote cactus. It has been used in Native American spiritual ceremonies for centuries. It is known for its ability to induce vivid and meaningful hallucinations.

Next, we will explore DMT, a naturally-occurring psychedelic substance found in plants and animals. It is typically vaporized or smoked for its powerful but short-lasting effects, which are known to induce intense and mystical experiences.

Lastly, we will look at ayahuasca, a traditional Amazonian brew made from the ayahuasca vine and other plants, known for its strong visual hallucinations and spiritual effects and increas-

Introduction

ingly being used in therapeutic settings for the treatment of various mental health conditions.

As we will discover throughout this book, each substance has unique properties that make them distinct. Understanding these specific properties can provide a deeper understanding of hallucinogens and their potential benefits for mental health and well-being.

Chapter 1

Lysergic Acid Diethylamide (LSD)

Lysergic acid diethylamide (LSD), also known as acid, blotter, dots, and yellow sunshine, is a powerful psychedelic substance that has been the subject of much controversy and debate throughout its history. Developed in 1938 by a Swiss chemist, Albert Hofmann, LSD is a synthetic compound known for its ability to alter perception, thoughts, and feelings in profound ways. The chemical structure of LSD is composed of a ring of four carbon atoms with a nitrogen atom and a diethylamide group attached. It acts on the serotonin receptors in the brain, specifically the 5-HT2A receptor, leading to the alteration of sensory perception, emotions, and thought processes.

In the 1950s and 60s, LSD became popular as a tool for self-discovery and personal growth and played a significant role in the counterculture movement of the time. However, as drug use and abuse increased, concerns about the safety and potential risks of LSD led to its criminalization in the 1970s. Since then, LSD has been classified as a Schedule I controlled substance in the United States, which means it is considered to have a high potential for abuse and no currently accepted medical use.

Despite its criminalization, LSD research has continued. Recent studies have suggested that it may have therapeutic potential for conditions such as cluster headaches, end-of-life anxiety, and alcoholism. This chapter will explore the chemical structure, effects on the brain, history, cultural significance, and therapeutic uses of LSD. It will also provide an in-depth understanding of the specific properties of this substance and its potential therapeutic benefits and risks.

Chemical Structure and Effects on the Brain

Lysergic acid diethylamide (LSD) is a synthetic compound known for its powerful and long-lasting hallucinations. It was first synthesized in 1938 by Albert Hofmann, a Swiss chemist, who is also credited with discovering the psychoactive effects of the compound.

The Power of Hallucinogens

The chemical structure of LSD consists of a ring of four carbon atoms with a nitrogen atom and a diethylamide group attached. The specific structure of LSD is what gives it its unique psychoactive properties. It acts on the serotonin receptors in the brain, specifically the 5-HT2A receptor. This leads to altered sensory perception, emotions, and thought processes.

LSD produces profound changes in consciousness, including perception, thought, and emotion. It can cause an individual to experience visual and auditory hallucinations lasting up to 12 hours or more. The effects of LSD can be highly variable and are influenced by factors such as dose, set, and setting. At low doses, the effects of LSD may be subtle. Still, at higher doses, the hallucinations can be vivid and intense.

The effects of LSD on the brain are still not fully understood, but research has begun to shed light on how this substance affects the brain. For example, studies have suggested that LSD affects how the brain processes information and increases communication between different brain regions. Studies have also shown that

LSD affects how the brain processes information from the eyes and increases brain plasticity.

In conclusion, LSD is a synthetic compound known for its powerful and long-lasting hallucinations. Its chemical structure and effects on serotonin receptors in the brain make it unique among other psychedelics. Despite its unique properties, the effects of LSD on the brain and its specific mechanisms of action are not fully understood. More research is needed to understand the full effects of LSD and its potential therapeutic benefits.

History and Cultural Significance

Lysergic acid diethylamide (LSD) was synthesized in 1938 by a Swiss chemist, Albert Hofmann while working for the pharmaceutical company Sandoz. At the time, the compound was intended to be used as a circulatory and respiratory stimulant. Still, it was soon discovered to have profound psychedelic properties. Hofmann discovered the compound's psychoactive effects after accidentally absorbing a small amount through his skin while working on the substance.

In the following years, LSD was widely used by scientists, artists, and the general public as a tool for self-discovery and personal growth. It was particularly popular in the 1950s and 60s when it became a central part of the counterculture movement. The counterculture movement embraced LSD to challenge traditional social norms, and the psychedelic experience was seen as a way to expand the mind and gain a new perspective on the world.

However, as drug use and abuse increased, concerns about the safety and potential risks of LSD began to rise. This led to the criminalization of LSD in the 1970s. It has been classified as a Schedule I controlled substance in the United States, which means it is considered to have a high potential for abuse and no currently accepted medical use.

The Power of Hallucinogens

Despite its criminalization, the use of LSD has not disappeared, and it continues to be used today in various contexts. From its historical significance as a powerful tool for self-discovery and personal growth to its cultural significance as a symbol of counterculture, LSD has played a significant role in shaping various aspects of society. Its impact can be seen in areas such as art, literature, music, and the field of psychology, where its use in research and therapy has led to new insights into the workings of the mind.

It's worth noting that recent studies and clinical trials conducted by various organizations and researchers looking into the therapeutic benefits of psychedelics have had positive results. It is promising in treating various mental health conditions such as depression, PTSD, addiction, and end-of-life anxiety. These renewed interests have led to an ongoing debate about the classification and legal status of psychedelics and their potential benefits for mental health and well-being.

Overall, the history and cultural significance of LSD is a

complex and multifaceted subject that spans several decades. From its initial discovery and early uses as a tool for self-discovery and personal growth to its criminalization and continued use today in recreational and therapeutic settings. It's still being debated, and its full potential is not yet understood. Still, the recent studies and research on the therapeutic benefits of psychedelics provide new insights into its use and impact on society.

Risks and Potential Therapeutic Uses

Lysergic acid diethylamide (LSD) is a powerful psychedelic substance, and its effects can be unpredictable. While it can produce profound changes in consciousness that may be beneficial in certain contexts, there are also risks associated with its use.

One of the primary risks of LSD is its ability to cause intense and vivid hallucinations that can be disorienting and overwhelming for some individuals. It can also increase the likelihood of experiencing anxiety, paranoia, and psychosis in some people, particularly those predisposed to such conditions. In addition, long-term use of LSD can lead to persistent psychosis, or "flashbacks," which can occur weeks or even months after the last dose. LSD can also cause physiological effects such as increased blood pressure, heart rate, and body temperature, which can be dangerous if not monitored properly.

Despite the negative risks, recent research has also shown potential therapeutic uses of LSD. Studies have suggested that it may be useful in treating conditions such as cluster headaches, end-of-life anxiety, and alcoholism. In addition, research also suggests that it may have a role in treating mental disorders such as depression and anxiety. However, more research is needed to understand the therapeutic benefits and risks of LSD fully. In addition, it's important to note that FDA does not approve LSD as a therapeutic agent. As such, its use for therapeutic purposes is highly restricted.

Finally, LSD is a powerful psychedelic substance with complex effects. While it has the potential to be therapeutic in certain conditions, it also has negative risks and potential for abuse. More research is needed to fully understand the benefits and risks of using LSD as a therapeutic agent. In addition, it should be used under the guidance of a trained medical professional in a controlled and safe environment.

A Guide to Taking LSD

LSD, also known as lysergic acid diethylamide, is a powerful psychedelic drug that can produce intense and profound changes in perception, thought, and emotion. It is available in various forms, including tablets, capsules, and liquids.

The recommended dosage for LSD is typically between 50 and 150 micrograms. However, it is important to remember that individual sensitivity to the drug can vary greatly. Hence, it is best to start with a lower dose and work your way up.

LSD can last anywhere from 6 to 12 hours or more, depending on the dose and the individual. The effects of the drug typically peak around 2-4 hours after ingestion and gradually decrease over the next several hours.

It is recommended to take LSD in a safe and comfortable environment, preferably with people you trust and with whom you feel comfortable. Some people prefer to take the drug outdoors in nature, while others prefer a more controlled setting, such as their own home.

Taking LSD safely involves being prepared for the potential psychological effects of the drug, as well as taking steps to minimize the risk of physical harm. This includes having a sober trip sitter present, staying hydrated, and avoiding dangerous activities while under the influence. It is also important to be aware that LSD can cause flashbacks, so it is best to avoid taking the drug if you have a history of mental health issues or are currently experiencing emotional distress.

It is illegal to consume, possess, and distribute LSD in most countries. Therefore, its possession, use, and distribution are criminal offenses. Therefore, it is important to consider the legal risks before deciding to take the drug.

It is also important to note that this information is for educational purposes only and is not intended as a substitute for professional medical advice, diagnosis, or treatment. It is not safe to take LSD, and one should always consult a healthcare professional before taking any drug.

In conclusion, lysergic acid diethylamide (LSD) is a powerful psychedelic substance with a unique chemical structure and mode of action. Its effects on the serotonin receptors in the brain can cause intense and long-lasting hallucinations that can alter perception, thoughts, and feelings.

Throughout history, LSD has played a significant role in shaping culture, art, literature, and music, as well as in the field of psychology. It was widely used as a tool for self-discovery and personal growth in the 1950s and 60s and played a central role in the counterculture movement of the time. However, as drug use and abuse increased, concerns about the safety and potential risks of LSD led to its criminalization in the 1970s.

Recent research suggests that when used in a controlled setting and under the guidance of trained professionals, LSD has potential therapeutic benefits for treating conditions such as cluster headaches, end-of-life anxiety, and alcoholism. However, it's important to note that more research is needed to understand the therapeutic benefits and risks of LSD fully. In addition, despite its potential therapeutic benefits, it's important to remember that the FDA does not yet approve LSD as a therapeutic agent, which poses risks to its users. As a result, it's important to use caution and fully understand the drug's effects before attempting to use it.

Chapter Summary

- Lysergic acid diethylamide (LSD) is a powerful psychedelic substance that profoundly alters perception, thoughts, and feelings.
- Developed in 1938 by a Swiss chemist, Albert Hofmann, LSD is a synthetic compound that acts on the serotonin receptors in the brain, specifically the 5-HT2A receptor.
- In the 1950s and 60s, LSD became popular as a tool for self-discovery and personal growth and played a

- significant role in the counterculture movement of the time.
- However, as drug use and abuse increased, concerns about the safety and potential risks of LSD led to its criminalization in the 1970s.
- Despite its criminalization, LSD research has continued. Recent studies have suggested that it may have therapeutic potential for conditions such as cluster headaches, end-of-life anxiety, and alcoholism.
- The effects of LSD can be highly variable and are influenced by factors such as dose, set, and setting. It can cause an individual to experience visual and auditory hallucinations lasting up to 12 hours or more.
- The effects of LSD on the brain are still not fully understood, but research has begun to shed light on how this substance affects the brain.
- More research is needed to understand the full effects of LSD and its potential therapeutic benefits.

Chapter 2

Psilocybin

Psilocybin, also known as magic mushrooms, shrooms, and psychedelic mushrooms, is a naturally occurring psychedelic compound found in certain species of mushrooms. The use of these mushrooms has been recorded for centuries in traditional shamanic and spiritual practices by indigenous cultures worldwide. However, it wasn't until the 1950s that psilocybin was first chemically synthesized, and Western scientists discovered its psychoactive properties.

Psilocybin works by acting on the serotonin receptors in the brain, specifically the 5-HT2A receptor, which alters sensory perception, emotions, and thought processes. It produces profound changes in consciousness, including perception, thought, and emotion. The effects of psilocybin can be highly variable and are influenced by factors such as dose, set, and setting.

In recent years, there has been renewed interest in studying the therapeutic potential of psilocybin, particularly for treatment-resistant depression, anxiety, and PTSD. However, despite the promising research, much remains to be understood about the specific mechanisms of action and risks associated with using psilocybin. This chapter will explore the chemical structure, effects on the brain, history, cultural significance, and therapeutic uses of psilocybin.

Chemical Structure and Effects on the Brain

Psilocybin is a naturally occurring psychedelic compound in certain mushrooms, most notably the Psilocybe genus. The chemical structure of psilocybin is composed of an indole ring, a basic structure found in many naturally occurring compounds, and a phosphorylated hydroxy group. This unique combination of elements is what gives psilocybin its psychoactive properties.

The Power of Hallucinogens

Psilocybin acts on the serotonin receptors in the brain, specifically the 5-HT2A receptor, which plays a critical role in regulating mood, emotion, and perception. The activation of the 5-HT2A receptors leads to changes in the neural activity in the brain, resulting in the alteration of sensory perception, emotions, and thought processes.

Psilocybin produces profound changes in consciousness and affective states, including changes in perception, thought, and emotion. As a result, it can cause an individual to experience visual and auditory hallucinations lasting up to 6 hours or more. The effects of psilocybin can be highly variable and are influenced by factors such as dose, set, and setting. At low doses, the effects of psilocybin may be subtle. Still, at higher doses, the hallucinations can be vivid and intense.

The effects of psilocybin on the brain are not fully understood. Still, research has begun to shed light on the mechanisms by which this substance affects the brain. For example, studies have suggested that psilocybin increases the connectivity between different brain regions, specifically between the default mode network involved in self-referential and reflective thinking and the task-positive network involved in perception, attention, and movement.

History and Cultural Significance

Psilocybin mushrooms have been used for centuries in traditional shamanic and spiritual practices by indigenous cultures worldwide. The use of these mushrooms has been depicted in rock paintings and artifacts, suggesting that their use is a longstanding tradition. The use of psilocybin mushrooms was primarily used for spiritual and medicinal purposes, allowing the shaman or spiritual leader to communicate with the spirit world, access altered states of consciousness, and diagnose and treat illnesses.

It was not until the 1950s that psilocybin was first chemically synthesized by Western scientists, and its psychoactive properties were discovered. This sparked a renewed interest in psilocybin and its potential medical uses among the scientific community. In the following decades, psilocybin research became popular among scientists. It was also used by counterculture movements, who embraced psychedelics as a tool for personal growth, self-discovery, and a way to challenge traditional social norms.

In recent years, there has been renewed interest in the therapeutic potential of psilocybin, particularly for treatment-resistant depression, anxiety, and PTSD. Studies have shown that the use of psilocybin in combination with therapy can lead to significant improvement in symptoms and overall well-being. It's a possible alternative treatment for patients who have not responded to traditional treatments. The recent trend of renewed interest in the study of psychedelics has led to a growing body of research on the therapeutic uses of psychedelics and their safety and efficacy for treating various mental health conditions.

Risks and Potential Therapeutic Uses

While psilocybin is considered less risky than other psychedelics, it still poses risks to the user. High doses can cause anxiety, paranoia, and other psychological distress. It's also important to note that consuming wild-picked mushrooms can be risky as some mushrooms can be toxic and cause serious harm or even death. Long-term use of psilocybin is also poorly understood and could have a negative impact.

However, research suggests that when used in a controlled setting and under the guidance of trained professionals, psilocybin has a range of therapeutic benefits. For example, studies have shown that psilocybin-assisted therapy can be effective in treating treatment-resistant depression and anxiety, as also PTSD. Furthermore, research suggests that psilocybin may have a therapeutic potential on other mental and physical conditions such as cluster headaches, addiction, and even end-of-life anxiety. Additionally, psilocybin could be used as an aid to psychotherapy, providing an opportunity for personal insight and emotional processing.

While the research is promising, more studies are needed to fully understand the therapeutic benefits and risks of psilocybin and the optimal dosing and administration methods. Despite the ongoing research and promising results, psilocybin is not yet an FDA-approved therapeutic agent and should be used only under the guidance of trained healthcare professionals. Moreover, it is important to be aware of laws and regulations, as psilocybin is a controlled substance in many countries.

A Guide to Taking Psilocybin

Psilocybin is a naturally occurring psychedelic compound found in certain species of mushrooms. It is often used for spiritual or therapeutic purposes. It is known for its ability to create profound changes in the user's perception, thoughts, and emotions. Here is a guide to taking psilocybin safely and effectively.

Psilocybin can be found in several forms, including fresh or dried mushrooms, capsules, or powdered extract. The mushrooms can vary in appearance, but they generally have a brown or tan cap and stem. Capsules and powdered extract are usually sold in small, labeled packages.

The amount of psilocybin needed can vary depending on the individual. Still, a typical starting dose is around 0.5-1.5 grams of dried mushrooms. However, it's important to start with a low dose and work your way up to avoid overwhelming effects.

The effects of psilocybin typically last around 4-6 hours or more, with the experience peak occurring around 2-3 hours after ingestion.

Psilocybin should be taken in a safe, comfortable, and familiar environment. A quiet, dark room or outdoor space can be ideal, as it allows for greater introspection and contemplation. However, it's important to avoid taking psilocybin in public or in an unfamiliar setting, as it can be disorienting and potentially dangerous.

Here are some important tips to keep in mind when taking psilocybin:

- Avoid combining with other substances, such as alcohol or other drugs, as this can increase the risk of negative side effects.
- Make sure you're in a good state of mind before taking psilocybin. Avoid taking it if you're feeling anxious, depressed, or stressed.
- Have a designated "sober" person to monitor you and ensure your safety.
- Be prepared for the possibility of intense emotional experiences or hallucinations.

- Remember that psilocybin can cause confusion and disorientation, so avoid driving or operating heavy machinery while under the influence.

Psilocybin is a powerful substance that can change the user's perception and emotions. To ensure a safe and effective experience, start with a low dose, take it in a comfortable and familiar environment, and have a designated "sober" person around to monitor your safety. With these guidelines in mind, you can experience the benefits of psilocybin while minimizing the risks.

In conclusion, psilocybin is a naturally occurring psychedelic compound found in certain mushrooms that have been used for centuries in traditional shamanic and spiritual practices by indigenous cultures. Its chemical structure and mode of action on the serotonin receptors in the brain can cause hallucinations and alter perception, thoughts, and feelings.

In recent years, there has been renewed interest in studying the therapeutic potential of psilocybin, particularly for treatment-resistant depression, anxiety, and PTSD. Studies have shown that Psilocybin-assisted therapy can effectively treat these conditions in a controlled setting and under the guidance of trained professionals. Research also suggests that it may be useful in addressing cluster headaches, addiction, and end-of-life anxiety.

While the therapeutic benefits of psilocybin are promising, it's important to remember that more research is needed to understand the therapeutic benefits and risks of psilocybin fully. In addition, the FDA does not approve it as a therapeutic agent, and consuming wild-picked mushrooms can be risky as some mushrooms can be toxic and cause serious harm. Therefore, it's important to use caution and fully understand the drug's effects before attempting to use it.

Overall, psilocybin is a unique substance that has a long history of traditional use and is showing promise in recent research for therapeutic applications. However, it is important to approach its use with care and caution.

Chapter Summary

- Psilocybin is a naturally occurring psychedelic compound found in certain species of mushrooms that have been used for centuries in traditional shamanic and spiritual practices by indigenous cultures worldwide.
- The chemical structure of psilocybin is composed of an indole ring and a phosphorylated hydroxy group, which gives it its psychoactive properties.
- Psilocybin works by acting on the serotonin receptors in the brain, specifically the 5-HT2A receptor, which alters sensory perception, emotions, and thought processes.
- The effects of psilocybin can be highly variable and are influenced by factors such as dose, set, and setting.
- In recent years, there has been renewed interest in studying the therapeutic potential of psilocybin, particularly for treatment-resistant depression, anxiety, and PTSD.
- The use of psilocybin mushrooms has been depicted in rock paintings and artifacts, suggesting that their use is a longstanding tradition. The use of psilocybin mushrooms was primarily used for spiritual and medicinal purposes.
- Psilocybin was first chemically synthesized by Western scientists in the 1950s, and its psychoactive

properties were discovered. This sparked renewed interest in its potential medical uses among the scientific community.

- In recent years, there has been renewed interest in studying the therapeutic potential of psilocybin, particularly for treatment-resistant depression, anxiety, and PTSD. However, much remains to be understood about the specific mechanisms of action and risks associated with using psilocybin.

Chapter 3

Mescaline (Peyote)

Mescaline, also known as peyote or "mesc," is a psychoactive alkaloid found in the peyote cactus. It has been used for centuries in the traditional spiritual practices of indigenous people in Mexico and the American Southwest. Mescaline is known for its ability to induce vivid and meaningful hallucinations. In addition, western scientists and artists have used it to explore the nature of consciousness.

In this chapter, we will explore the chemical structure and effects of mescaline on the brain, its history and cultural significance, and its potential therapeutic uses and risks. Understanding the specific properties of this substance and its potential benefits can provide a deeper understanding of the broader topic of psychedelics.

Chemical Structure and Effects on the Brain

Mescaline, also known as 3,4,5-trimethoxyphenethylamine (or 3,4,5-TMPEA for short), is a naturally occurring psychoactive alkaloid found in the peyote cactus (Lophophora williamsii) and other cacti species. It is known for its ability to induce vivid and meaningful hallucinations, as well as its ability to change the way an individual perceives the world.

Mescaline's chemical structure consists of a phenethylamine core, a type of organic compound found in many naturally occurring substances, with a methoxy group attached to the nitrogen R_3 and an isopropyl group attached to the nitrogen R_2. The specific arrangement of atoms in the molecule gives it its unique psychoactive properties.

When consumed, mescaline acts on the serotonin receptors in the brain, specifically the 5-HT2A receptor, responsible for regulating mood, perception, and cognitive processes. This leads to altered sensory perception, emotions, and thought processes.

Depending on the individual, the effects can vary depending on the dosage and can last anywhere from 8 to 12 hours.

At low doses, the effects of mescaline can be subtle. They may include changes in perception of colors and shapes and a heightened sense of well-being and euphoria. At higher doses, the hallucinations can be vivid and intense. They may include changes in perception of time and a sense of interconnectedness with the world. Additionally, mescaline may have potential therapeutic uses for treating certain mental health conditions like depression, anxiety, and PTSD. Still, it's important to note that more research is needed to understand the therapeutic benefits and risks of the substance fully.

History and Cultural Significance

The use of mescaline and the peyote cactus holds deep cultural and spiritual significance for indigenous people, who have used it for centuries in traditional ceremonies and rituals. The peyote cactus, also known as the "sacred cactus," is central to the belief systems and religious practices of many indigenous tribes. In addition, its use is often seen as a way to connect with the spiritual world and gain a deeper understanding of one's place.

In addition to its traditional use, Western scientists and artists have also widely studied mescaline. In the early 20th century, mescaline was used in experimental psychology and psychiatry as a tool to explore the nature of consciousness and perception. Researchers believe the psychedelic experiences induced by mescaline provide insight into the workings of the human mind. They used it in research on schizophrenia and other mental disorders.

The counterculture movement of the 1950s and 60s also embraced mescaline and other psychedelics to challenge traditional social norms and expand the mind. During this time, mescaline was used by artists and writers as a tool for self-expression and creativity. However, as with other psychedelics, mescaline's increasing use and abuse led to concerns about its safety and potential risks.

In conclusion, mescaline is a psychoactive alkaloid known for its ability to induce vivid and meaningful hallucinations. Its use has deep cultural and spiritual significance for indigenous people and has played a significant role in Western science and counter-culture history. Understanding mescaline's cultural significance and history are crucial to fully understanding its effects on human consciousness and potential therapeutic uses.

Risks and Potential Therapeutic Uses

While mescaline is considered relatively safe, with few negative side effects when used in traditional, controlled settings, its effects can vary depending on the individual, the dosage, and the setting in which it is consumed. For example, high doses can lead to anxiety, paranoia, and psychological distress. Furthermore, as with any psychedelic substance, there is a risk of having a "bad trip," which can lead to lasting negative psychological effects.

Despite the lack of scientific research, traditional use of peyote cactus and anecdotal evidence suggest potential therapeutic benefits of mescaline. Some studies have suggested that mescaline-assisted therapy may be useful in treating addiction, depression, anxiety, and PTSD. Research also suggests that it may have a role in treating cluster headaches and end-of-life anxiety. More controlled, rigorous research is needed to understand mescaline's therapeutic benefits and risks fully, and it is not approved as a therapeutic agent by the FDA. It's important to note that consuming wild-harvested peyote may be risky as it could be misidentified or contaminated.

A Guide to Taking Mescaline

Mescaline is a psychedelic substance found in certain cacti, most notably the peyote cactus. It can also be synthesized in a laboratory. The substance is typically consumed by ingesting the cactus but can also be consumed in powder or capsule form.

When taking mescaline, it is important to know that the effects can vary depending on the dose consumed. A moderate dose can range from 200-500mg, while a heavy dose can be over 1000mg. The effects of mescaline typically last for 8-12 hours.

It is important to take mescaline in a safe and comfortable environment, ideally with people you trust. A safe and comfortable setting will help to minimize the risk of a bad trip or other negative reactions.

It is also important to remember that mescaline can produce intense hallucinations and alter your perception of reality, so it is important to have a clear state of mind and be in a state of well-being before consuming it.

As with any psychedelic substance, it is important to start with a low dose and work your way up, as the effects can be unpredictable. It is also essential to be aware that the use of mescaline is illegal in many places. Hence, it is important to be aware of the laws in your area.

It is also important to be aware that mescaline can interact with other medications you might be taking, so it is essential to consult with a doctor or a medical professional before consuming it.

In summary, mescaline is a powerful psychedelic substance that can be consumed in various forms. Before taking it, it is important to be aware of the dosage, the duration of the effects, the environment, and the risks. Taking it in a safe and comfortable place with people you trust and a clear state of mind is important. Please consult with a doctor or a medical professional before consuming it.

In conclusion, mescaline is a psychoactive alkaloid found in the peyote cactus that has a long history of use in traditional spiritual practices by indigenous cultures. It's known for its ability to induce vivid and meaningful hallucinations. In addition, its effects on the brain, specifically on serotonin receptors, lead to altered sensory perception, emotions, and thought processes. Despite its historical use, there is limited scientific research on the therapeutic benefits of mescaline. However, studies have suggested its potential therapeutic benefits for treating addiction, depression, and anxiety. Still, more research is needed to understand mescaline's therapeutic benefits and risks fully. Additionally, it's important to note that mescaline is not an FDA-approved therapeutic agent and should be used under the guidance of trained professionals. However, mescaline's cultural and historical significance cannot be denied, adding a unique dimension to understanding its effects and potential future use.

Chapter Summary

- Mescaline, also known as peyote, is a psychoactive alkaloid found in the peyote cactus.
- It has been used for centuries in the traditional spiritual practices of indigenous people in Mexico and the American Southwest.
- Mescaline is known for its ability to induce vivid and meaningful hallucinations.
- Mescaline's chemical structure is a phenethylamine core, with a methoxy group attached to the nitrogen R_3 and an isopropyl group attached to the nitrogen R_2.
- Mescaline acts on serotonin receptors in the brain, specifically the 5-HT2A receptor, which is responsible for regulating mood, perception, and cognitive processes.
- The effects of mescaline can vary depending on the dosage and can last anywhere from 8 to 12 hours.
- The use of mescaline and the peyote cactus holds deep cultural and spiritual significance for indigenous people.
- Western scientists and artists have also widely studied mescaline in the early 20th century as a tool to explore the nature of consciousness and perception. The counterculture movement of the 1950s and 60s also embraced mescaline and other psychedelics.

Chapter 4
N,N-Dimethyltryptamine (DMT)

N,N-Dimethyltryptamine, also known as DMT, Dimitri, The Spirit Molecule, Businessman's Trip, Dimenstyline, and N,N-DMT, is a naturally-occurring psychedelic substance in various plants and animals. This powerful substance is known for its intense and mystical effects, often described as profound and life-changing. Due to its unique properties, DMT has gained much attention in neuroscience and psychotherapy.

In this chapter, we will take a closer look at the chemical structure of DMT and how it interacts with the brain. We will also explore DMT's historical and cultural significance, including its use in traditional spiritual practices. Furthermore, we will examine the potential therapeutic benefits of DMT, including its use in treating addiction, PTSD, and other mental health conditions.

However, it is important to note that DMT is not without risks. The use of DMT can lead to adverse effects, including hallucinations, paranoia, and even psychosis. Therefore, it is essential to approach the use of DMT with caution and to be fully informed about the potential risks and benefits associated with its use.

As we delve deeper into this topic, we will better understand the unique properties of DMT and its place in the broader world of psychedelics. Despite the potential risks, the therapeutic benefits of DMT warrant further research and investigation. Understanding the chemical structure, effects on the brain, historical and cultural significance, therapeutic benefits, and risks associated with DMT can help us make more informed decisions about its use.

Chemical Structure and Effects on the Brain

N,N-Dimethyltryptamine (DMT) is a naturally-occurring psychedelic substance found in many plants and animals, including certain species of trees, shrubs, and mushrooms. Its chemical structure is composed of a tryptamine molecule with a

The Power of Hallucinogens

dimethyl group attached to the nitrogen atoms, which gives it its unique psychoactive properties. DMT acts on the serotonin receptors in the brain, specifically the 5-HT2A receptor, leading to the alteration of sensory perception, emotions, and thought processes.

DMT is typically vaporized or smoked for its powerful and short-lasting effects. Its onset is rapid, and the effects can be intense and profound. The experience can include vivid visual hallucinations, profound changes in thought and emotion, and a sense of euphoria. In addition to its powerful hallucinations, DMT is also known to induce mystical and spiritual experiences. Some users have reported experiencing a sense of transcendence and connection to a higher power. The duration of the effects of DMT is relatively short, usually lasting around 30-60 minutes.

DMT is considered one of the most powerful psychedelics. However, its effects can be highly variable and are influenced by dose, set, and setting factors. While DMT is considered relatively safe, it can also pose some risks to the user. For example, high doses can cause anxiety, paranoia, and other psychological distress. In addition, some users may experience psychologically distressing effects known as "bad trips." Therefore, it's important to use DMT under the guidance of trained professionals in a controlled setting.

History and Cultural Significance

DMT has a long history of use in traditional spiritual practices by indigenous cultures in South America. It is consumed in the form of a brew called ayahuasca. However, its use in the Western world began in the 1950s. It was popularized by writers such as Terence McKenna and Rick Strassman, who wrote extensively about their experiences with the substance.

DMT has also been used in various spiritual and religious practices worldwide, with different cultures having unique ways of consuming it. The effects of DMT are considered to be profound. They can include intense and vivid hallucinations and feelings of transcendence. It is known to produce mystical experiences, and some users report encountering entities or otherworldly beings. DMT has been associated with various spiritual practices, including meditation, shamanism, and ceremonial rituals.

DMT has also played a role in the counterculture movement of the 1960s and 1970s. It was considered a powerful tool for self-discovery and personal growth. Many artists and musicians used it to access new forms of creativity. DMT has also been studied by scientists and researchers who have sought to understand its effects on the brain and consciousness.

Criminalized in the 1970s, DMT is considered a Schedule I controlled substance in the United States, with no accepted medical use and a high potential for abuse. However, recent studies have shown the potential therapeutic benefits of DMT, particularly in treating addiction and PTSD, but research is still ongoing.

Risks and Potential Therapeutic Uses

DMT, while considered to be relatively safe in terms of physical risks, its effects on the mind can be intense and potentially distressing for some individuals. High doses or long-term use can lead to persistent psychosis or "flashbacks," which can occur weeks or even months after the last dose. It's also important to note that DMT is a Schedule I controlled substance. Therefore, it is illegal to manufacture, possess, or use DMT in most countries.

However, in recent years, research has begun to explore the potential therapeutic benefits of DMT. For example, studies have suggested that DMT-assisted therapy may be useful in treating addiction, PTSD, and depression. Additionally, DMT has been used in spiritual and therapeutic settings to achieve personal growth and self-discovery. However, research on the therapeutic benefits of DMT is still in its early stages, and more research is needed to understand its potential therapeutic uses and risks fully.

Lastly, DMT is a naturally-occurring psychedelic substance with a long history of use in traditional spiritual practices. Its chemical structure, effects on the brain, historical and cultural significance, potential therapeutic uses, and risks make it a fascinating subject to study. While more research is needed to understand the therapeutic benefits of DMT fully, and it is not legal and not an approved therapeutic agent by FDA, it has the potential for further exploration in the mental health and well-being field.

A Guide to Taking DMT

DMT is a powerful psychedelic substance that can produce intense and profound experiences. It can be found in various forms, including powder, crystals, and liquid, and can be ingested, vaporized, or injected.

The appropriate dosage of DMT varies depending on the form, method of consumption, and individual tolerance. A typical oral dosage is between 20-40 milligrams, while vaporization typically requires a lower dose of around 10-20 milligrams. Therefore, it's important to start with a low dosage and gradually increase it to avoid overwhelming experiences or negative reactions.

A DMT experience can vary but typically lasts around 30-60 minutes when vaporized and 1-2 hours when consumed orally.

When taking DMT, it's important to have a comfortable and safe environment. It's recommended to have a trusted sitter present and avoid taking DMT in public or where you feel unsafe.

The safety of DMT use largely depends on the method of consumption, dosage, and individual tolerance. It can have serious short-term and long-term effects on mental and physical health when consumed in high doses or when mixed with other substances. Therefore, before consumption, it is important to research the substance and its positive and negative effects. It is also important to remember that DMT is a Schedule I controlled substance in the United States and many other countries, and possession and use are illegal.

It is important to remember that the effects of psychedelics can vary greatly from person to person, and it is important to approach them with caution and care. As always, it's best to consult a healthcare professional before consuming any substance.

. . .

In conclusion, DMT is a naturally-occurring psychedelic substance found in plants and animals used for centuries in traditional spiritual practices. Its chemical structure consists of a tryptamine molecule with a dimethyl group at the nitrogen positions, which allows it to interact with serotonin receptors in the brain and produce intense and mystical experiences.

Despite its long history of use in traditional settings, scientific research on the effects of DMT on the brain is still limited. However, studies have suggested that DMT may have therapeutic potential in treating certain conditions such as addiction, PTSD, and depression. However, more research is needed to understand DMT's potential benefits and risks fully. In addition, it's important to note that DMT is illegal in many countries and not approved as a therapeutic agent by the FDA.

Overall, the study of DMT provides insight into the complex and unique effects of psychedelics on the human mind and consciousness. Further research on the potential therapeutic uses of DMT could lead to new treatments for mental health conditions and a deeper understanding of the nature of consciousness.

Chapter Summary

- N,N-Dimethyltryptamine (DMT) is a naturally-occurring psychedelic substance found in many plants and animals, including certain species of trees, shrubs, and mushrooms.
- Its chemical structure is composed of a tryptamine molecule with a dimethyl group attached to the nitrogen atoms, which gives it its unique psychoactive properties.
- DMT acts on the serotonin receptors in the brain, specifically the 5-HT2A receptor, leading to the

alteration of sensory perception, emotions, and thought processes.
- DMT is typically vaporized or smoked for its powerful and short-lasting effects, including vivid visual hallucinations, profound changes in thought and emotion, and a sense of euphoria.
- DMT has a long history of use in traditional spiritual practices by indigenous cultures in South America and was popularized by writers in the Western world in the 1950s.
- DMT has played a role in the counterculture movement of the 1960s and 1970s and has been studied by scientists and researchers to understand its effects on the brain and consciousness.
- DMT is considered a Schedule I controlled substance in the United States, with no accepted medical use and a high potential for abuse. Still, recent studies have shown the potential therapeutic benefits of DMT, particularly in treating addiction and PTSD.
- DMT, while considered to be relatively safe in terms of physical risks, its effects on the mind can be intense and potentially distressing for some individuals. They should be used under the guidance of trained professionals in a controlled setting.

Chapter 5

Ayahuasca

In this chapter, we will delve into the fascinating world of ayahuasca—a traditional Amazonian brew used for centuries by indigenous people for spiritual, medicinal, and ceremonial purposes. The brew, made from the ayahuasca vine (Banisteriopsis caapi) and other plants, is known for its powerful psychedelic effects and is believed to possess a wide range of therapeutic benefits.

We will explore the history and cultural significance of ayahuasca, its chemical composition, and its effects on the brain. Additionally, we will examine the potential therapeutic uses of ayahuasca and the risks associated with its use. The chapter also will include recent research developments in the field and the legal status of ayahuasca. By the end of this chapter, you will have a comprehensive understanding of this fascinating brew and its place in modern society.

Chemical Structure and Effects on the Brain

Ayahuasca, a traditional Amazonian brew, combines the ayahuasca vine (Banisteriopsis caapi) with other plants, particularly the leaves of the chacruna plant (Psychotria Viridis), which contain the powerful psychedelic compound DMT. This brew has been used for centuries by indigenous people for spiritual and medicinal purposes.

The chemical composition of ayahuasca is particularly noteworthy, as it contains two key ingredients that interact in the body to produce its psychoactive effects. The first active ingredient is DMT, a naturally-occurring compound known to produce strong visual hallucinations and a sense of euphoria and spiritual transcendence. The second active ingredient is MAOIs (Monoamine oxidase inhibitors), which are found in the ayahuasca vine.

When consumed, DMT and MAOIs interact with the brain in unique ways. DMT works by binding to serotonin receptors in the brain, which releases other neurotransmitters that alter the perception of reality. Conversely, the MAOIs inhibit the breakdown of neurotransmitters, allowing DMT to remain active in the body for longer periods.

Combining these two ingredients creates a powerful synergy that produces various psychological and perceptual effects associated with ayahuasca. The brew is known to elicit a broad range of emotions, which can range from a profound sense of euphoria and well-being to feelings of intense fear and anxiety. The exact nature of the effects of ayahuasca can depend on the dose consumed, the context in which it is consumed, and the individual's state of mind and prior experiences.

Due to its strong psychoactive effects, ayahuasca has been the subject of much scientific research. It is considered to have potential therapeutic applications in psychiatry and psychology. Despite this, the use of ayahuasca is controversial, and its legal status varies from country to country.

History and Cultural Significance

Ayahuasca, a traditional Amazonian brew, has a rich and complex history that spans centuries of use by indigenous people in the region. The brew is considered to be a sacred medicine. It has been used for various purposes, including spiritual, medicinal, and ceremonial practices. Indigenous people believe that ayahuasca can connect with the spirit world, achieve spiritual insight and understanding, and access hidden knowledge and wisdom.

The use of ayahuasca has been passed down through generations and has deep cultural roots in indigenous communities. It is often used in traditional ceremonies that are steeped in ritual and symbolism and which are considered to be powerful and transformative experiences. The use of ayahuasca is closely tied to indigenous people's spiritual beliefs and practices, and it is seen as an essential part of their traditional way of life.

In the 20th century, the use of ayahuasca began to spread

outside of the Amazon region, particularly in the Western world. As more people became interested in the brew and its potential benefits, it began to be used in various new contexts. For example, in the Western world, ayahuasca has been used in spiritual and therapeutic settings as a tool for self-discovery and personal growth and to treat various mental health conditions.

The cultural significance of ayahuasca is reflected in the growing number of people who travel to the Amazon to participate in traditional ceremonies to gain a deeper understanding of the indigenous culture and its practices. In addition, the popularity of ayahuasca tourism has increased awareness of the brew and its potential benefits and raised several ethical questions about commercializing traditional practices.

The scientific community is increasingly recognizing the cultural significance of ayahuasca. Studies on the neuropsychopharmacology of ayahuasca have revealed that it can be used as a tool for healing and self-discovery and plays an important role in preserving the cultural heritage of the Amazonian people. In recent years, ayahuasca has also gained the attention of scientists, anthropologists, and other researchers studying its use and the benefits it can provide.

Risks and Potential Therapeutic Uses

While considered a powerful and transformative tool, ayahuasca carries certain risks and potential dangers. For example, consuming ayahuasca can lead to psychological distress in some individuals, including anxiety, paranoia, and intense hallucinations. It's also important to note that, while physical risks are considered to be low when consumed under the guidance of a trained facilitator, long-term use or high doses of ayahuasca can lead to persistent psychosis, or "flashbacks," which can occur for weeks or even months after the last dose.

Furthermore, certain medications may interact negatively with ayahuasca, such as antidepressants and blood thinners, and they should not be combined with those medications. Moreover, it's not recommended for people with a history of serious mental illnesses and other medical conditions, so it's important to consult a healthcare professional before consumption.

Despite its risks, ayahuasca has also been studied for its potential therapeutic benefits. Studies have suggested that ayahuasca-assisted therapy may be useful in treating conditions such as addiction, PTSD, and depression. Research has also suggested that it may have benefits for treating symptoms of anxiety, depression, and PTSD in individuals with treatment-resistant conditions. Additionally, ayahuasca is being researched for its potential to help alleviate symptoms of PTSD, anxiety, and depression.

However, research on the therapeutic benefits of ayahuasca is still relatively limited, and more studies are needed to understand its potential benefits and risks fully. In many countries, ayahuasca is considered a Schedule I drug, and it's illegal to possess, consume or sell it. However, in some other countries, it's regulated and used in therapeutic contexts. Additionally, it's not approved by the FDA as a therapeutic agent. Therefore, it's important to be aware of the legal status of ayahuasca in one's country and only uses it under a trained professional's guidance.

A Guide to Taking Ayahuasca

Ayahuasca is a powerful psychoactive brew traditionally used by indigenous people in the Amazon region for spiritual and healing purposes. It is typically made by boiling the ayahuasca vine (Banisteriopsis caapi) and the leaves of the chacruna plant (Psychotria Viridis) together.

Different forms of ayahuasca can vary in color, consistency, and strength, but typically the liquid is dark brown and thick. The taste is often described as bitter and unpleasant.

The recommended dosage of ayahuasca varies depending on the individual and the specific brew used. It's important to start with a small dose and gradually increase it to find your comfort level. It's also important to be guided by an experienced facilitator.

The effects of ayahuasca can last anywhere from 4 to 8 hours. It can cause intense hallucinations, changes in perception, and powerful emotional experiences.

Ayahuasca ceremonies are typically held in a traditional setting, such as a maloca (a large round thatched-roof building) in the Amazon jungle. However, it can be taken in other settings, such as a retreat center or a private ceremony.

Safety is a major concern when taking ayahuasca. Therefore, working with a qualified and experienced facilitator or shaman who can provide guidance and support throughout the experience is important. Additionally, it's important to avoid certain medications, such as antidepressants and blood thinners, and to inform the facilitator of any pre-existing medical conditions. It's also important to be in a safe and comfortable environment and to have a trusted sitter or guide who can assist you during the experience.

It's also important to note that ayahuasca is illegal in some countries, and it's important to check the laws in your area before attempting to take it.

In conclusion, ayahuasca is a traditional Amazonian brew used for centuries by indigenous people for spiritual, medicinal, and ceremonial purposes. Its unique chemical composition, containing DMT and MAOIs, allows for powerful psychedelic effects on the brain. Research has suggested potential therapeutic uses for addiction, PTSD, and depression. Still, more research is needed to understand the benefits and risks associated with its use fully.

The cultural significance of ayahuasca reflects the growing number of people who travel to the Amazon to participate in traditional ceremonies, heal themselves, and understand the indigenous people's spiritual and ceremonial practices. However, it's also important to note that ayahuasca carries certain risks, including psychological distress and potential negative interactions with certain medications, and should only be consumed under the guidance of a trained professional.

Ayahuasca is a complex substance with many potential benefits and risks. This chapter aims to provide a comprehensive overview of the history, cultural significance, chemical composition, effects, therapeutic uses, and risks associated with ayahuasca to help readers understand this fascinating brew. However, it's important to remember that even though ayahuasca has a lot of potential benefits, it's only recommended for some, and one should be aware of its legal status and the potential risks before consuming it.

Chapter Summary

- Ayahuasca is a traditional Amazonian brew made from the ayahuasca vine and other plants. It is known for its powerful psychedelic effects and is believed to possess therapeutic benefits.
- The brew's chemical composition includes the active ingredient DMT, a naturally-occurring compound known to produce strong visual hallucinations and a sense of euphoria, and MAOIs (Monoamine oxidase inhibitors) found in the ayahuasca vine.
- When consumed, DMT and MAOIs interact with the brain uniquely, releasing other neurotransmitters that alter the perception of reality.
- The effects of ayahuasca can range from euphoria to intense fear and anxiety, depending on the dose, context, and individual's state of mind.
- Ayahuasca has potential therapeutic applications in psychiatry and psychology. Still, its use is controversial, and its legal status varies by country.
- Ayahuasca has a rich history of use by indigenous people for spiritual, medicinal, and ceremonial purposes. It is considered a sacred medicine with deep cultural roots.
- In the 20th century, ayahuasca began to spread outside of the Amazon region, particularly in the Western world, where it is used in spiritual and therapeutic contexts.

Chapter 6

Personal Stories

This chapter focuses on personal stories of individuals who have used psychedelics, specifically lysergic acid diethylamide (LSD), psilocybin, mescaline (peyote), N,N-dimethyltryptamine (DMT), and ayahuasca for various purposes.

These stories offer a unique and personal perspective on the effects of these substances on the mind and how they can be used for personal growth, therapy, spiritual exploration, and other purposes. Through the stories, you will be able to understand the diversity of experiences and the potential benefits and risks of using psychedelics.

Ultimately, this chapter serves as a window into the subjective experience of these individuals and the profound ways in which psychedelics can impact one's life and consciousness.

Stories About LSD

John's Story of Using LSD for Personal Growth

John had always been deeply invested in personal development, constantly seeking new and innovative ways to improve himself and gain a greater understanding of the world around him. As he delved deeper into this pursuit, he became increasingly curious about the effects of psychedelics on the mind and the potential benefits they could offer those seeking self-improvement.

After much research and contemplation, John finally decided to take the plunge and try LSD for the first time under the guidance and supervision of a trained professional in a safe and controlled setting. He was aware of the potential risks and hazards but also felt confident in his readiness and ability to handle the experience.

As soon as the LSD took effect, John knew he was in for something special. The world around him seemed to take on a whole new dimension, and he felt his mind opening up to new and previously unimaginable possibilities. He described the experience as profound and transformative, allowing him to gain insight into his thought patterns and behaviors in ways he could never have imagined.

Through the journey, John felt like he was able to overcome personal barriers and achieve a greater sense of self-awareness. The insight and understanding he gained from experience allowed him to see his life and himself in a new light. They helped him to navigate the path of personal growth with more grace and ease. He felt that the LSD experience had been a crucial step in his self-discovery journey, and he has been grateful for the opportunity to explore the inner workings of his mind in such a profound way.

Sarah's Experience With LSD-Assisted Therapy

Sarah had been dealing with the debilitating effects of anxiety and depression for many years. Despite her best efforts, she could not find lasting relief through traditional therapy and medication. She had exhausted all the options and was feeling hopeless and at a loss as to what to do next. That's when she learned about LSD-assisted therapy as a potential alternative.

At first, Sarah was skeptical and hesitant. She had heard the stories about the dangers and risks associated with LSD, and she wasn't sure if this was a path she wanted to take. But the more she researched, the more she learned about the promising results of this form of therapy. So finally, she saw it as a possible last resort worth exploring.

Sarah was under the guidance of a trained therapist, who

helped her prepare for the therapy sessions and explained the process at every step. As a result, she felt comfortable in a safe and controlled environment and could relax and trust the process.

As soon as the LSD took effect, Sarah felt her mind start to open up. She found that the LSD helped her to see her thoughts and emotions from a new perspective and that it helped her to process and understand them differently. In addition, the therapy sessions unlocked a door inside her mind, allowing her to access and confront parts of herself that she had been trying to avoid or suppress.

Sarah reported feeling more relaxed and at ease after the therapy sessions. She found that her depression and anxiety symptoms had greatly improved and that she had gained a greater understanding and insight into her struggles. She was grateful for the opportunity to try LSD-assisted therapy and saw it as a life-changing experience that helped her regain control of her mental and emotional well-being.

Stories About Psilocybin

Michael's Journey Using Psilocybin for Spiritual Exploration

Michael had always been fascinated by spirituality and the search for meaning and purpose in life. However, he had struggled to find a traditional practice or belief system that truly resonated with him and felt like it fit. He had tried many different approaches over the years. Still, nothing seemed to give him the depth of understanding and connection he was searching for.

In his quest for something deeper, Michael first learned about the potential of psychedelics, specifically psilocybin, as a means of exploring spirituality. He had heard stories of others having profound spiritual experiences. At the same time, under the influence of these substances, he was intrigued by the possibility that it could be a way for him to access the deeper understanding and connection he was searching for.

After much research and contemplation, Michael decided to take the plunge and try psilocybin in a formal setting with a trained guide. He wanted to approach the experience with the utmost respect and reverence, and he felt this was the best way to do so.

As soon as he consumed the psilocybin, Michael entered a profound and mystical experience. He felt his mind opening up to new and previously unimaginable possibilities and a deep sense of connection with a deeper sense of self and the universe. He described the experience as transformative, allowing him to gain insight into his thought patterns and behaviors in ways he could never have imagined. In addition, he felt he could tap into a sense of interconnectedness and oneness that he had never experienced before.

Through the journey, Michael found that the experience helped him better understand himself and his place in the world. He felt like he had been given a new perspective on his existence and that he had gained a deeper understanding of the spiritual nature of reality. In addition, he had found a new way of connecting to a spiritual dimension, which helped improve his life. He felt that the psilocybin experience had been a crucial step in his spiritual journey, and he's been grateful for the opportunity to explore the inner workings of his mind and soul in such a profound way.

The Power of Hallucinogens

Emily's Account of Using Psilocybin to Overcome PTSD

Emily had been living with the debilitating effects of Post-Traumatic Stress Disorder (PTSD) for several years. Despite her best efforts, she could not find lasting relief through traditional therapy and medication. Instead, she has tried different types of therapy, such as cognitive-behavioral and talk therapy. Still, she found that they did not help her to address the root cause of her PTSD. She had exhausted all the options and was feeling hopeless and at a loss as to what to do next. That's when she learned about psilocybin-assisted therapy as a potential alternative treatment for PTSD.

At first, Emily was skeptical and hesitant. She had heard the stories about the dangers and risks associated with psychedelics, and she wasn't sure if this was a path she wanted to take. But the more she researched, the more she learned about the promising results that had been achieved with this form of therapy, particularly for those with PTSD. So finally, she saw it as a possible last resort worth exploring.

Emily was under the guidance of a trained therapist, who helped her prepare for the therapy sessions and explained the process at every step. As a result, she felt comfortable in a safe and controlled environment and could relax and trust the process.

As soon as the psilocybin took effect, Emily felt her mind start to open up. She found that psilocybin helped her to process and understand her traumatic memories differently. It allowed her to gain insight and understanding into the root causes of her PTSD and helped her to let go of the negative thoughts, emotions, and memories associated with her traumatic experiences. In addition, the therapy sessions unlocked a door inside her mind, allowing her to access and confront parts of herself that she had been trying to avoid or suppress.

Emily reported feeling more relaxed and at ease after the therapy sessions. She found that her PTSD symptoms had greatly improved and that she had gained a greater understanding and insight into her struggles. She was grateful for the opportunity to try psilocybin-assisted therapy and saw it as a life-changing experience that had helped her overcome the negative impact of her traumatic experiences on her life and regain control of her emotional well-being.

Stories About Peyote

Scott's Account of Using Peyote in a Native American Ceremony

Scott had always been drawn to the rich culture and spiritual practices of Native American tribes. He had spent many years studying and learning about their ways of life. He had always felt a deep connection to the natural world. He believed that the traditional practices of these ancient cultures held many answers to his questions about the meaning and purpose of existence.

As part of his ongoing quest to learn more about Native American spirituality, Scott decided to participate in a peyote ceremony led by a traditional Native American medicine man. Peyote is a small, spineless cactus with the psychoactive alkaloid mescaline, which has been used for centuries by indigenous people of North America for spiritual and ceremonial purposes.

The ceremony took place throughout the night, and other participants and traditional songs and prayers accompanied Scott. He was honored to be allowed to participate in such a sacred and meaningful ceremony. He approached the experience with humility and respect.

As soon as he consumed the peyote, Scott felt himself entering into a realm of profound and spiritual experience. He felt his mind opening up to new and previously unimaginable possibilities and a deep connection with the natural world and himself. He described the experience as transformative, allowing him to gain insight into his thought patterns and behaviors in ways he could never have imagined. In addition, he felt he could tap into a sense of interconnectedness and oneness that he had never experienced before.

Through the journey, Scott felt like he had been given a new perspective on his existence and that he had gained a deeper understanding of the spiritual nature of reality. He felt like he had been able to connect with the natural world in a way that was deeper and more meaningful than he had ever thought possible. He felt that the peyote ceremony had been a crucial step in his spiritual journey. He felt grateful for the opportunity to participate in such a sacred and meaningful ceremony. In addition, he was honored to have been able to connect with the teachings of the ancient indigenous cultures of North America.

Rachel's Experience With Peyote in a Therapeutic Setting

Rachel had been struggling with addiction for many years. Despite her best efforts, she could not find lasting relief through traditional therapy and medication. Instead, she has tried different types of therapy, such as cognitive-behavioral and talk therapy. Still, she found that they did not help her to address the root cause of her addiction. She had exhausted all the options and was feeling hopeless and at a loss as to what to do next. That's when she learned about peyote-assisted therapy as a potential alternative treatment for addiction.

At first, Rachel was skeptical and hesitant. She had heard the stories about the dangers and risks associated with psychedelics, and she wasn't sure if this was a path she wanted to take. But the more she researched, the more she learned about the promising results that had been achieved with this form of therapy, particularly for those with addiction. She began to see it as a possible last resort worth exploring.

Rachel was under the guidance of a trained therapist, who helped her prepare for the therapy sessions and explained the process at every step. As a result, she felt comfortable in a safe and controlled environment and could relax and trust the process.

As soon as the peyote took effect, Rachel felt her mind start to open up. She found that the peyote helped her to understand the root causes of her addiction and the underlying emotional and psychological factors that had led to it. It allowed her to gain insight into her addiction and the patterns of thoughts and behaviors that had kept her trapped in its cycle. The therapy sessions unlocked a door inside her mind, allowing her to access and confront parts of herself that she had been trying to avoid or suppress.

Rachel reported feeling more in control of her life after the therapy sessions. She found that her addiction symptoms had greatly improved and that she had gained a greater understanding and insight into her struggles. She was grateful for the opportunity to try peyote-assisted therapy and saw it as a life-changing experience that helped her overcome her addiction and regain control of her life.

Stories About DMT

David's Ecounter With an "Entity" During a DMT Trip

David had always been deeply interested in the realm of psychedelics and the potential benefits they could offer for exploring the nature of consciousness and the self. He had read extensively about the various substances and their effects. He had always been particularly intrigued by DMT's powerful and intense effects.

After much research and contemplation, David finally decided to take the plunge and try DMT for himself, under the guidance and supervision of a trained professional in a safe and controlled setting. He was aware of the potential risks and hazards but also felt confident in his readiness and ability to handle the experience.

As soon as the DMT took effect, David knew he was in for something special. He described the experience as intense and otherworldly. He felt as though he had been transported to a completely different dimension. As the trip progressed, he felt like he had encountered an "entity" or intelligent being communicating with him in a language he couldn't understand. David felt like the entity had shared deep insights and knowledge with him. He felt like the entity was trying to convey important information. Still, the language barrier prevented him from fully understanding.

David felt that the experience had been deeply meaningful and transformative and had changed his perspective on life and consciousness in ways he could never have imagined. He felt that the DMT experience had helped him gain a new understanding of reality and the nature of existence. It had opened his mind to new and unimaginable possibilities. He felt that the experience was a glimpse into the hidden depths of reality and consciousness.

It left him with a sense of wonder and awe about the world and our place.

Samantha's Use of DMT to Connect With Nature

Samantha had always felt a profound connection to nature. She had always found solace and inspiration in the beauty of the natural world. From an early age, she had been drawn to the outdoors, spending much of her free time hiking, camping, and exploring the wilderness.

As she got older, Samantha began to feel the desire to explore this connection to nature more profoundly. As a result, she became curious about the potential benefits of psychedelics. In particular, she had heard about DMT's powerful and transformative effects and felt that it might deepen her connection to nature in ways she had never experienced before.

After much research and contemplation, Samantha decided to take the plunge and try DMT for herself in the most natural setting, surrounded by the beauty of nature that could be a place for her to immerse into the DMT experience fully. She found a place where she felt comfortable and could relax and trust the process.

As soon as the DMT took effect, Samantha felt her connection to nature intensifying and felt like she had been transported to a different realm. The beauty of the natural world became even more vivid and intense, and she felt as though she had connected with the natural world in a new and deeper way. She described the experience as profound and felt that it helped her to understand the interconnectedness of all things and the oneness of nature.

Samantha felt that the experience had strengthened her

connection to nature and her sense of self. She felt that the DMT experience had helped her understand reality and the nature of existence and opened her mind to new and unimaginable possibilities. She felt that the experience was a glimpse into the hidden depths of reality and consciousness. It left her with a sense of wonder and awe about the world and our place. She felt that the experience had helped her to deepen her appreciation and understanding of the natural world and to reconnect with the beauty of the natural world in a way that was deeper, more meaningful, and more profound than she had ever thought possible.

Stories About Ayahuasca

The Power of Hallucinogens

Anthony's Journey to Healing Through the Ayahuasca Ceremony

Anthony had been struggling with addiction for many years. Despite his best efforts, he could not find lasting relief through traditional therapy and medication. He had tried different types of therapy, such as cognitive-behavioral and talk therapy, as well as support groups and 12-step programs. Still, he found that they did not help him address his addiction's root cause. He had exhausted all of the available options and was feeling hopeless and at a loss as to what to do next.

That's when he heard about ayahuasca, a powerful psychedelic plant medicine used for centuries by indigenous people of the Amazon for spiritual and healing purposes. He learned about its potential for helping individuals overcome addiction and other psychological issues and was deeply intrigued by the idea of using it to heal.

Anthony decided to participate in an ayahuasca ceremony led by a traditional shaman who had decades of experience working with the medicine. He knew that this would be a powerful and potentially challenging experience. Still, he was determined to do whatever it took to overcome his addiction and find lasting healing.

The ceremony took place in a traditional setting, and other participants and traditional songs and prayers accompanied Anthony. As soon as he drank the ayahuasca brew, he felt himself entering a realm of intense and emotional experience. He felt like the ayahuasca helped him to confront and overcome the root causes of his addiction by allowing him to understand the underlying emotional and psychological factors that had led to it.

Anthony felt that the ceremony helped him to gain a greater sense of self-awareness and control. He felt that he had a better understanding of himself and his addiction and that he had been able to let go of the negative thoughts, emotions, and memories that had kept him trapped in the cycle of addiction. He felt he had been given the tools and insights to take control of his healing and move forward positively.

During the ceremony, he felt like he had been able to connect with his innermost self and gain a deeper understanding of the origins of his addiction. He felt like he could see things from a different perspective, allowing him to see the patterns and behaviors that had led him to addiction and kept him trapped. He felt that the ayahuasca had given him the courage and strength to confront these patterns and behaviors head-on and start healing.

After the ceremony, Anthony felt a sense of renewed hope and optimism. He felt that he had been given a second chance and that he had been given the tools and insights he needed to start building a better life for himself. He felt like he had been given a new perspective on his addiction and that he had gained a deeper understanding of himself and the world around him. He was grateful for the opportunity to participate in the ayahuasca ceremony. He felt it had been a life-changing experience that helped him overcome his addiction and regain control of his life.

Gina's Account of Ayahuasca-Assisted Therapy for Depression

Gina had been struggling with depression for many years. Despite her best efforts, she could not find lasting relief through traditional therapy and medication. Instead, she tried different types of therapy, such as cognitive-behavioral therapy and talk therapy. Still, she found that they did not help her to address the root cause of her depression. She had exhausted all the options and was feeling hopeless and at a loss as to what to do next.

That's when she heard about ayahuasca-assisted therapy as a potential alternative treatment for depression. She learned about how ayahuasca had helped other people understand and process their feelings of depression in a new way and was deeply intrigued by the idea of using it as a means of healing.

Gina decided to participate in ayahuasca-assisted therapy led by a trained therapist, who helped her prepare for the therapy sessions and explained the process at every step. As a result, she felt comfortable in a safe and controlled environment and could relax and trust the process.

As soon as the ayahuasca took effect, Gina felt her mind start to open up. She found that the ayahuasca helped her to understand and process her feelings of depression in a new way by allowing her to gain insight and understanding into the underlying emotional and psychological factors that had led to it. It helped her to understand her depression more deeply and to see it from a different perspective.

Gina reported feeling more positive and hopeful after the therapy sessions. She found that her depression symptoms had greatly improved and that she had gained a greater understanding and insight into her struggles. She was grateful for the opportunity to try ayahuasca-assisted therapy and saw it as a life-changing experience that had helped her to overcome her depression and take back control of her life.

The therapy sessions also helped her to gain a greater understanding of the interconnectedness of all things. The ayahuasca had given her a deeper understanding of the mind-body connection, how emotions and thoughts are connected, and how they affect her overall well-being. This understanding helped her to have a more holistic approach to her healing journey. As a result, she felt she had more tools and insights to address her depression from different angles.

In conclusion, the personal stories in this chapter provide insight into the different effects of the drugs discussed in the book. They add to understanding these substances' potential therapeutic uses and cultural significance. Each story is unique and reflects the individual's personal experience and perception. Still, together they paint a broader picture of the effects and implications of these substances. It's important to note that these substances should be used with caution and should always be conducted under the guidance of a trained professional in a safe and controlled setting.

Afterword

The book delves into the complex and often-misunderstood topic of hallucinogens, focusing on five specific substances: LSD, psilocybin, mescaline (peyote), DMT, and ayahuasca. Each substance is unique and has distinct properties, brain effects, and history.

Starting with LSD, also known as lysergic acid diethylamide, the book examines the chemical structure and how it interacts with the brain to produce vivid hallucinations and profound changes in perception. The book also covers the history of LSD, including its initial discovery in the 1940s, its widespread use in the 1950s and 1960s, and its eventual criminalization in the 1970s.

Next, the book delves into psilocybin, a chemical found in certain species of mushrooms. Psilocybin is structurally similar to serotonin, a neurotransmitter in the brain. It is believed to play a role in regulating mood, perception, and other cognitive processes. The book also covers the history of psilocybin, including its use in traditional indigenous cultures and its recent resurgence in research as a potential therapeutic tool.

Mescaline (peyote) is a naturally occurring psychoactive compound in the peyote cactus. The book covers its chemical

Afterword

structure and effects on the brain and its traditional use in indigenous cultures of Mexico and the southwestern United States.

DMT (N,N-dimethyltryptamine) is a powerful psychedelic drug structurally related to serotonin. The book describes the effects of DMT on the brain and consciousness, its history and cultural significance, and its traditional use in Amazonian shamanic practices.

Lastly, ayahuasca is a brew traditionally used by indigenous people of the Amazon basin. It is made from the ayahuasca vine and chakruna leaves. The book covers the history and cultural significance of ayahuasca, its use in traditional shamanic practices, and its chemical composition and effects on the brain.

In addition to providing information on these substances' physical and historical aspects, and a guide to taking them safely, the book also includes personal accounts of individuals who have used these substances for personal growth, spiritual exploration, and therapeutic purposes. Through these accounts, the book aims to provide a nuanced and well-rounded understanding of these substances' potential risks and benefits. Ultimately, this book aims to foster a deeper understanding and appreciation of these powerful and complex substances and their potential role in human consciousness and well-being.

Overview of Current Research and Areas for Future Study

Recent years have seen an increase in research on the therapeutic uses of hallucinogens. A growing body of evidence suggests that these substances may have potential benefits for treating various mental health conditions. Studies have been conducted using psychedelics such as LSD, psilocybin, and ayahuasca to treat addiction, post-traumatic stress disorder (PTSD), depression, and anxiety. These studies have generally been small-scale, but they

Afterword

have produced promising results. As a result, they have generated significant interest in further research.

Despite this progress, there is still much that remains unknown about the therapeutic uses of hallucinogens. To fully understand the benefits and risks of these substances, large-scale, well-designed clinical trials are needed. These trials should include long-term follow-up to determine treatment effects' durability and active comparison, groups. Additionally, research is needed to understand the optimal dosing, frequency, and duration of treatment.

One key area that requires further research is the mechanisms of action of these substances. While we know that psychedelics interact with the serotonin system in the brain, we do not fully understand how these interactions lead to the changes in perception and consciousness associated with the psychedelic experience. Additional research is needed to identify the specific neural pathways and receptors involved in psychedelics' therapeutic effects.

Furthermore, more research must be conducted on these substances' cultural and spiritual significance. They have been used in traditional and indigenous cultures for centuries, often as part of religious or spiritual practices. However, while these substances may have an important role in these cultures, there is a limited scientific understanding of the mechanisms behind these cultural and spiritual uses, so future research could investigate the cultural and spiritual aspects of these substances by studying their use in traditional or indigenous cultures.

While research on the therapeutic uses of hallucinogens is progressing, much is still to be learned. Additional research is needed to confirm the findings of initial studies, to understand the optimal dosing and administration of these substances, and to fully understand the mechanisms of action and potential risks associated with their use. With continued research, we can gain a

Implications for Society and Policy

The potential therapeutic benefits of hallucinogens have significant implications for society and policy. As discussed in the book, these substances have the potential to be used to treat a variety of mental health conditions, such as addiction, PTSD, and depression. However, due to their current Schedule I controlled substances classification, it isn't easy to research their therapeutic potential. This can make it challenging to fully gather the necessary data to understand their benefits and risks and develop effective and safe treatments. Additionally, this classification can criminalize individuals who use or possess these substances for personal growth or therapeutic reasons.

Given the current state of research, it's important to consider a more nuanced and evidence-based approach to regulating these substances. This could include reclassifying certain substances, such as psilocybin, as Schedule IV controlled substances, which have a lower potential for abuse and are considered to have a currently accepted medical use. This would allow for more research to be conducted and protect individuals who use these substances for therapeutic purposes.

Furthermore, it is important to recognize that this substance could have different levels of risk and benefits. Therefore, different regulations can be applied. Not all Hallucinogens are equal in terms of risk and benefits. Therefore, reclassifying and regulating some substances differently from others might be appropriate.

This book has provided a comprehensive overview of hallucinogens, including their chemical structure and effects on

Afterword

the brain, history and cultural significance, risks, potential therapeutic uses, and a guide to taking them safely. It has also highlighted the importance of further research and a more nuanced approach to regulating these substances. As research continues to evolve, it's crucial to consider the implications of these findings for society and policy. This includes the need to reclassify certain substances, adjust regulations to allow for further research, and ensure that individuals who use these substances for therapeutic purposes are protected.

Acknowledgments

Writing this book would not have been possible without the help and support of many individuals. First, I would like to extend my heartfelt gratitude to my family and friends, who have always been there for me, providing unwavering support and encouragement throughout the writing process.

I am deeply grateful to the experts and researchers in the field of psychedelics and hallucinogens who have shared their knowledge and insights with me. Their contributions have been invaluable in helping me to understand the subject matter better.

I would also like to acknowledge the individuals who shared their personal experiences and stories with me. Their candid and honest accounts have added a unique and personal perspective to the book.

I also want to thank my editor, who helped me to refine my work and make it the best it could be.

Finally, I would like to thank all the readers who took the time to read this book. This book will contribute to a better understanding of these fascinating and powerful substances and their potential benefits for mental health and well-being.

About the Author

Terence Wright is a researcher, writer, and expert on psychedelics, focusing on hallucinogens' effects and cultural significance. He has studied the subject for several years and has published several articles on the topic. Terence has a deep passion for understanding how psychedelics have been used throughout history and how they can be used in the future. He is an advocate of the responsible use of psychedelics. He believes that with more research and understanding, these substances can positively impact mental health and well-being. When not writing or researching, he enjoys hiking and spending time with his family.

***

Dear fellow psychonauts,

Thank you for embarking on this journey of exploration with me. I trust that you found my book on the history, effects, and cultural significance of these five beautiful hallucinogens to be an insightful and thought-provoking read. If you found the book valuable, please leave a review on the platform where you purchased it. Your feedback would help others discover the book and help me continue to share knowledge on the topic of psychedelics.

Sincerely, Terence Wright

www.ingramcontent.com/pod-product-compliance
Lightning Source LLC
Chambersburg PA
CBHW072103110526
44590CB00018B/3299